Original title:
Through the Palm Fronds

Copyright © 2025 Creative Arts Management OÜ
All rights reserved.

Author: Lucas Harrington
ISBN HARDBACK: 978-1-80581-499-3
ISBN PAPERBACK: 978-1-80581-026-1
ISBN EBOOK: 978-1-80581-499-3

Refuge Beneath Nature's Arms

In the shade where the critters play,
Lizards lounge in a sunlit ballet.
Squirrels plotting with nutty schemes,
Laughing softly at the humans' dreams.

A breeze brings tickles, a flutter of leaves,
As I dodged a dive-bomb from a bird that believes,
This is his fortress, his kingdom to rule,
While I sip lemonade and try not to drool.

Breezes Carrying Ancient Whispers

Winds tell secrets of the long-lost days,
Of dancers in grass with grasshopper ways.
A whispered joke from a rustling stem,
Oh, how I chuckle at nature's whim!

Clouds giggle softly in the summer glow,
As I pretend to be a nature show pro.
Birds mimic laughter with chirps and flaps,
While I trip on roots with giggling claps.

Colors of Life in Hidden Spaces

In the nooks where the colors collide,
A painter's palette mixed with pride.
Bees are buzzing their buzz-worthy tune,
While flowers nod and say, "Make room!"

Rainbow socks on a toad's tiny feet,
Jumping on gumdrops, oh, what a feat!
Every bloom's got a silly tale,
Behind blooming laughter, I can't help but bail!

Melodies Woven with Green Threads

A symphony plays in a rustling choir,
Frogs are the stars, they never tire.
Crickets dance under a disco moon,
While I two-step and hope I'll swoon.

The leaves are the instruments, shaking and swaying,
As the stars above join in the playing.
In this jam session, I am the fool,
Grooving along in my makeshift pool!

Symphony Beneath the Tropical Canopy

The monkeys play their xylophones,
While toucans cheer with shrill tones,
A frond whispers jokes to the air,
As lizards strut with flamboyant flair.

The iguana steals a mango treat,
While parrots dance on happy feet,
A squirrel laughs at the show's delight,
As shadows swirl in the fading light.

Beneath the Canopy's Embrace

The breeze tells tales of mischief done,
As leaves giggle in the playful sun,
A sloth drags slowly, grinning aloof,
While frogs leap high — oh, what a goof!

A raccoon dons a leafy crown,
As butterflies twirl, never down,
Beneath the cover, laughter spins,
In nature's jest, everyone wins!

Reflections of Light and Leaf

Sunlight pirouettes on emerald screens,
As critters plot their cheeky schemes,
Mischief dances in dappled beams,
As laughter flows like the wildest dreams.

Grasshoppers hum in a jazzy beat,
While shadows tap in a funky feat,
The antics of worms in a wormy waltz,
Bring chuckles forth, as laughter exalts.

Tangles of Nature's Affection

Vines play tag with the breeze so light,
While critters cavort from morn till night,
Chirping crickets claim the mic,
In this leafy world where all delight.

A parrot squawks a comical line,
While lizards boast of their sunlit shine,
From branches high, the laughter flows,
In tangled joy, life oddly glows.

The Lushness of Silent Conversations

In the garden where gossip grows,
Plants whisper secrets with a pose.
Cacti lean in with pointed grins,
While daisies chuckle at passers' sins.

The corn stalks gossip about the rain,
While sunflowers spin tales of pain.
A lettuce leaf flirts with a beet,
In this verdant world, life's never discreet.

A shy sprout blushes at the breeze,
As bushes shake their quippy knees.
Every petal knows a juicy plot,
Nature's chatter is a tangled knot.

So if you find yourself in the green,
Listen closely, join the scene.
For laughter blooms in leaves so bright,
In this leafy theater, pure delight.

Fluttering Stories in the Green

Breezes carry tales, old and new,
From fluttering wings, we hear the brew.
A butterfly jokes with a wandering bee,
As flowers giggle, 'Come sit with me!'

The crickets chirp in a merry band,
While a snail moves slow, taking a stand.
A tiny ant claims it found a crumb,
And everyone laughs, 'Oh, look who's numb!'

Branches shrug in a playful dance,
Swaying with joy in an open trance.
The trees debate whose shade is best,
While critters take turns in a feathered jest.

Nature's stage is filled with cheer,
Whimsical stories linger near.
A tapestry woven in vibrant green,
Where whimsical laughter is always seen.

The Language of Swaying Shadows

When shadows mingle in the afternoon,
They dance around like a playful tune.
The sunbeams laugh, casting cheeky grins,
As trees engage in some shadowy sins.

A clumsy squirrel trips over a root,
The shadows chuckle, finding it cute.
Leaves wag their tongues like gossiping friends,
As whispered jokes become pixelated bends.

The flowers sway, nodding in jest,
In this garden, humor's the best.
A raccoon winks from behind a bush,
And shadows ripple with a gentle hush.

Even the clouds join the fun of it,
Trading jokes as they casually flit.
In this symphony of light and dark,
Joyful giggles leave an endless mark.

Mosaic of Shade and Sunbeam

Under the oak, a cool mix of light,
Sunbeams tease the shade, what a delight!
Birds in chorus share their puns,
While the wind takes a swing, just for fun.

A beetle rolls by, making his claim,
'I'm the hottest one, what's your game?'
While daisies grumble about their space,
In this patchwork quilt, it's a lively race.

Branches wave like they've found a beat,
As flowers declare, 'We can't be beat!'
Leaves flip-flop in a whimsical chatter,
Where laughter is served on a silver platter.

The mosaic shines with colors so bold,
Stories leak out as the sunshine unfolds.
In this vibrant scene, no cares at all,
The world is a stage, come join the ball!

Treetop Serenades

Up above where squirrels play,
A bird croons in a comical sway.
Leaves dance to a goofy tune,
As shadows twist beneath the moon.

Laughter echoes, a monkey's prank,
Swinging low from a leafy flank.
Breezes tickle the froggy crew,
Jumping high for a silly view.

Sunbeams and Swaying Spirits

Sunlight spills like giggling gold,
On branches twisted and unrolled.
A chubby raccoon slips by with flair,
Decked in the day's party wear.

The wind whispers jokes to the trees,
As squirrels mimic dancing bees.
With shadows prancing in joy's embrace,
Nature's comedy finds its place.

The Flutter of Nature's Veil

Butterflies tease in a dizzying race,
While bees bump in a merry chase.
A lizard's smile gives quite the cheer,
As crickets break out in wild jeer.

Dancing leaves play peek-a-boo,
Under skies of the bluest hue.
A breeze carries laughter up high,
As all nature plays a sly guy.

Lush Reveries in Green

In the heart of bright leafy trails,
Frogs tell jokes with croaks that sails.
A tiny mouse makes quite the fuss,
In his search for the big, juicy crust.

The trees wear ribbons of vine and cheer,
As party hats for squirrels appear.
Bouncing life makes the shadows tangle,
In nature's laughter, we all dangle.

Traces of a Gentle Wind

A breeze whispers softly, plays a prank,
Leaves giggle and dance, an unseen flank.
Branches sway wildly, in an awkward show,
While squirrels roll by, putting on a row.

With each little gust, a tickle in tow,
Grass blades do the cha-cha, in a row.
Birds squawk in delight, making silly sounds,
As I trip on my own feet, lost on the grounds.

Laughter erupts, from the bushes nearby,
A raccoon pokes out, gives me a sly eye.
Nature's a jester, living full of glee,
In this raucous humor, where all are free.

Underneath Nature's Tapestry

Under the canopy, shadows frolic,
Colors swirl bright, oh what a comic.
Leaves wave goodbye, whispering low,
While ants take their coffee, putting on a show.

A turtle sneezes, sends a leaf soaring,
A critter's eye-wink, leaves me exploring.
Spider webs giggle, as they trap the sun,
Here in this tapestry, we all have fun.

Frogs croak a tune, very out of key,
A chorus of giggles springs forth from a tree.
Nature's a circus, with laughs in the air,
Beneath its great fabric, no need for a care.

Chasing Light Among the Leaves

Light dances in circles, like a puppy at play,
Chasing it around, oh what a ballet.
Leaves throw glimmers, quite the sight,
As I tumble and roll, feeling delight.

The sun winks at me, as if to say,
"Join the fun, child, don't just stay."
Butterflies flutter, in costumes so bright,
While I chase my shadow, an amusing plight.

A breeze tickles cheeks, sends hats on a spree,
I chase after one, thinking it's funny.
A squirrel joins in, with a mischievous glance,
Together we whirl, in this wacky dance.

Harmony in the Tropical Breeze

In the tropical sway, all things convene,
Monkeys laugh loudly, they're quite the scene.
Coconuts drop, like surprise party balls,
I dodge and I weave, hear nature's calls.

The parrots are squawking, it's quite a chat,
Chants of mischief, 'Have you seen my hat?'
Fruits drop like jokes, ripe and profound,
In laughter, we find where the fun's always found.

A lizard struts by, wearing shades for his feat,
With style so bold, can't accept defeat.
The breeze holds the melody, soft yet alive,
In this silly jungle, we all will thrive.

Nature's Gentle Sway

In the breeze, the leaves do dance,
Like they're caught in a silly trance.
Funny faces, shadows cast,
Nature's giggle but never fast.

Watch the fronds, they play and sway,
Like children teasing all day.
Whispers of fun in each green twist,
Sunshine grins, they can't resist.

The lizards laugh, they join the fun,
Frogs leap high, oh what a run!
A playful choir, nature's song,
In this light, we all belong.

With every breeze, a tickle here,
Nature's joke we hold so dear.
So let us dance and leap about,
In this world, there's never doubt.

Sylvan Whispers and Delicate Embrace

Amid the trees, a secret hides,
Where silliness in silence bides.
Leaves gossip softly, hey, did you hear?
The squirrel's antics are quite severe!

In this embrace of greenery bright,
Laughter echoes, a pure delight.
Branches shake, a joyful play,
Nature's shenanigans on display.

A butterfly stumbles, oh what a sight,
But it gets up, flutters, takes flight.
With every flap, it sends a cheer,
Nature's charm is perfectly clear.

The shadows giggle under the sun,
As critters frolic, oh what fun!
In the woods, no worries align,
Life's a jest in this grand design.

Harmony of Leaf and Light

Under the canopy, a dance so bright,
Leaves flutter down, like confetti in flight.
The sun peeks in with a wink and a grin,
While shadows play tag, let the games begin!

Twisting and twirling, a leafy ballet,
Nature's performance don't dare delay.
Frogs in tuxedos, they jump in surprise,
At the rustling laughter that fills the skies.

A wise old owl watches with glee,
As grasshoppers hop, oh, look at me!
Each moment a jest, each breeze a chance,
In this whimsical world, we all can dance.

So let the light shine, let the fun grow,
In this leafy wonder, we'll steal the show.
With each gentle sway, a chuckle is born,
In harmony bright, we greet the dawn.

The Secret Life of Leaves

What secrets do the leaves all share?
In whispers soft, they plot and dare.
Their little stories, woven in green,
Has anyone ever seen such a scene?

They gossip about the wind so bold,
And how the flowers don't do what they're told.
Every flutter, a wink, a cheeky jest,
Nature's comedy, oh what a fest!

The insects giggle, flitting around,
In this leafy world, joys abound.
Swinging in the breeze, no care in sight,
They'll keep you laughing from day to night.

So listen closely to the rustling fun,
Their shenanigans shine like the sun.
Under the canopy, the laughter weaves,
In the secret life led by the leaves.

The Whispering Dance of Dappled Light

Sunlight giggles in the breeze,
As shadows tango with the trees.
Leaves swap jokes in vibrant hues,
While squirrels debate the best of views.

Pigeons prance on branches high,
A feathered choir sings a lie.
They gossip loud, and none disband,
While ants march on, a tiny band.

Bikini-clad sunbeams take a dive,
Trying hard to stay alive.
With every shift, a brown dog snorts,
While light shows off in playful shorts.

Yet under all the lively din,
A sleepy turtle dreams of sin.
Unbothered still, he takes a nap,
On his shell, a leafy cap.

Colorful Visions in the Wilderness

Crickets chirp in rhythmic rhyme,
While frogs croak jokes to pass the time.
A butterfly in polka dots,
Winks at clowns in tangled knots.

The river flows with giddy glee,
It dances past the bumblebee.
Sunflowers grin from every row,
At the sunflower petal show.

Caterpillars throw a rave,
With disco balls, they misbehave.
A grasshopper leads them in a jig,
While fireflies flash, they dance a gig.

Above a tree, a raccoon spies,
On all the fun with gleaming eyes.
He wishes he could join the game,
But his fur coat's not the same!

Shelter of the Gentle Giants

In the shadow of the mighty oak,
Squirrels gather, sharing yolk.
They swap tales of acorn finds,
And pull pranks on passing minds.

The trunk laughs with creaky sound,
As rabbits hop and spin around.
A turtle in his shell so sly,
Pretends not to hear their lie.

The woodpecker knocks a tune,
Making all feel like a loon.
While deer prance in a graceful line,
Their secret is they're hard to find.

Giggles echo all around,
As the forest plays its sound.
In this haven, joy abounds,
Mother Nature's laugh resounds.

Echoing Lullabies of Nature

The wind sings soft, it can't keep quiet,
Whispers dreams, a joyful riot.
Crickets strum their tiny guitars,
Making tunes under the stars.

Badgers snore with little snorts,
While owls throw late-night sport reports.
The moon's a joker in the sky,
Throwing smiles as the night goes by.

Mice hold parties in the grass,
As fireflies flash, they shake their sass.
Each rustle hides a dance, a tease,
While everyone is up to mischief, please!

Nature's giggle, sweet and mild,
Cradles every curious child.
In the warmth of soft moonlight,
Every laughter takes its flight.

Whispers of Sunlit Shadows

Sunbeams dance on leafy heads,
A squirrel's bravado, stolen breads.
The shadows giggle, play hide and seek,
As birds crack jokes that make us weak.

Laughter echoes through the green,
Where mischief lurks, unseen, serene.
A lizard slips with comic flair,
Poking fun at the lazy bear.

Breezes swirl with cheeky grins,
Tickling toes of frolicking kin.
The sun winks down, a playful star,
As shadows hop, not straying far.

In this patch of joyous play,
Life's a sketch, a bright bouquet.
With every breeze, a chuckling tune,
Underneath the laughing moon.

Beneath the Canopy's Embrace

Under the green, we plot and scheme,
The sun's a jokester, a playful dream.
A turtle jokes, 'I may be slow,'
As rabbits race, putting on a show.

The breeze whispers secrets of silly sights,
Like owls who wear funny-looking tights.
Leaves chuckle softly, swaying with glee,
As I dance along, feeling so free.

An acorn drops, a bumbling fall,
The forest erupts in laughter, a call.
A raccoon rolls, all arms and fluff,
In this tapestry of fun, we can't get enough.

We sip on giggles beneath the shade,
In the heart of nature, joy is made.
The sun and moon share a playful fight,
While shadows join the dance, day and night.

Secrets in the Breeze

Whispers float on the gentle air,
A sloth croons songs, beyond compare.
The breeze tells tales of silly fears,
Like how frogs jump when a squirrel nears.

Laughter quakes through branches high,
As butterflies ponder how to fly.
A tiny ant wears a leaf like a hat,
Strutting proudly, fancy and fat.

The wind plays jokes with a rustling sound,
While blossoms giggle as they spin 'round.
The chattering brook sings silly rhymes,
As the sun grins wider, caught in its primes.

In this place where secrets weave,
Life's a jest, just watch and believe.
A dance of humor in every breeze,
Life unfurls, like laughter from trees.

Dancing Leaves in the Twilight

Leaves shimmy down as night draws near,
With twilight whispers, nothing to fear.
A cat does a jig, tail high and proud,
While crickets chirp, drawing a crowd.

Fireflies twinkle, donning their glow,
While shadows hide, putting on a show.
A raccoon prances with comic flair,
Inviting all to join the fair.

With moonlit beams, the fun ignites,
The world becomes a stage of delights.
As branches sway with the rhythm of jest,
And the heartbeat of twilight feels truly blessed.

In this carnival of shadow and light,
Where joy embraces the coming night.
With laughter echoing through the trees,
Life's a party, and we dance with ease.

Shadows Beneath Tropical Skies

In a world where lizards wear tiny shoes,
And monkeys play jazz while sipping on brews,
The sun's rays tickle the grass below,
With shadows dancing, putting on a show.

A toucan tells jokes, oh what a delight,
While squirrels recite poetry, taking flight,
Pineapple hats and coconuts in hand,
We laugh as the sunlight shifts in the sand.

Where palms gossip softly in the warm breeze,
And the world slows down with giggles and wheezes,
The days blend brightly, with humor we thrive,
In nature's comedy, we feel so alive.

So here's to the green in the sun-kissed air,
With laughter that's swirling like wild tropical hair,
Underneath the gleam where the wild things roam,
In this wacky paradise, we find our home.

Dancing Light in Foliage

The light plays tricks like a child at the park,
As shadows tango, igniting a spark,
The leaves wiggle and giggle in sweet embrace,
While critters are hiding, making a face.

A breeze whispers secrets, oh what a tease,
As butterflies engage in a game of freeze,
With laughter echoing from tree to tree,
The hilarity blooms like a sweet jubilee.

Fronds sway like dancers at a candy parade,
While sunlight spills candies, a sugary cascade,
A parrot croons ballads, a sassy old chap,
As nature spins tales in a zany mishap.

In foliage thick, we find humor abounds,
Among the wild whispers and playful sounds,
The glow of the day brings laughter anew,
In this playful paradise, there's joy to imbue.

Lush Veils of Sunlight

When sunlight drapes over the forest floor,
Like a silly magician, it leaves us wanting more,
The vines hang low, like outrageous hats,
While butterflies question the style of the rats.

Fronds wave hello with a cheeky grin,
Inviting mischief to dance from within,
Chasing the shadows like a playful cat,
Caught in the moment, we giggle at that.

The scene is a party, no plans to make,
As nature crafts humor with every mistake,
With giggling streams and a ticklish breeze,
In the lush of this world, we laugh with ease.

Beneath leafy canopies, jokes intertwine,
With sunlight as punchlines that endlessly shine,
In this green-hued escapade, joy never strays,
We're wrapped in laughter for the sunniest days.

Enchanted Fronds at Twilight

As twilight unfolds with an elegant wink,
The fronds tell stories that make us all think,
Mischievous shadows tiptoe across grass,
While owls crack jokes as the daylight will pass.

Hushed giggles ripple as fireflies ignite,
The woods come alive with delightfully bright,
In the space of whimsy, all worries float by,
As creatures concoct an elaborate pie.

The crickets join in with their symphonic groan,
Creating a tune that feels perfectly grown,
Beneath twinkling stars in their velvety veils,
We revel in laughter, we dance and we sail.

So here's to the twilight, to fronds we adore,
With every soft chuckle, we cherish much more,
In this enchanted eve, our spirits will play,
As the night paints adventures in a humorous way.

Tresses of the Tropical Wind

The wind rode in, a merry prank,
Tugging hats from heads, oh what a rank!
Palm fronds slapping, giggles abound,
As coconut squirrels dance around.

Monkeys swing, their disco moves,
They climb and tease, in playful grooves.
The sunbeam giggles, what a fun sight,
While palm trees swish, day turns to night.

Dreams Caught Between Leaves

A leaf fell down, with whispered schemes,
It caught a nap, in woven dreams.
Lizards strike poses, a comedy act,
While clouds above chuckle, that's a fact!

Frogs in tuxedos sing in the rain,
Hoping for fame, and a little refrain.
The breeze shakes laughter, a playful tease,
As napping daisies wave with ease.

Colorful Canvases of Nature's Hand

A painter came, with colors so bright,
Splashing green leaves, oh what a sight!
Tropical blooms, like clowns in a row,
Winking at bees, who steal the show.

Rainbows drip down from the skies,
While butterflies gossip and share their highs.
Nature's palette, a whimsical game,
With every stroke, nothing's the same.

Hidden Pathways in the Greenery

Behind the leaves, where shadows play,
Squirrels host parties, hip-hip-hooray!
With acorns abound, they munch and cheer,
Their laughter ringing, just so near.

The path winds on, with twists and turns,
Where each step taken, a new tale churns.
A raccoon juggles, just for fun,
While fireflies flicker, the night's begun.

The Soliloquy of Green Shadows

Amid the branches, laughter plays,
A squirrel wearing shades, having its phase.
Leaves gossip wildly, making a scene,
As sunshine tickles, all things turn green.

A bird's outburst, a comical song,
Shatters the calm, it cackles along.
Frogs interrupt with their quirky grins,
Who knew that nature held such wins?

The rustling palms join in a dance,
Inviting all life to take a chance.
Breezes giggle, with a playful sway,
To join this show, don't hesitate, hey!

So here we dwell, in our lively patch,
Where the shade and silliness always match.
Nature's jokes subtly cast their nets,
In green shadows, joy is where it sets.

Nature's Conductor of Light

Waving wands of emerald hue,
The sunbeams giggle, 'Look at you!'
Busting moves in playful style,
Nature leads with a cheeky smile.

The dance of light flips and sways,
As lizards strut with sunny rays.
Flowers burst out, colors collide,
In this concert, there's no need to hide.

Breeze, the maestro, shuffles about,
With whispers that leave no room for doubt.
Every leaf, a note on the score,
In harmony, nature opens the door.

The laughter of shadows joins the band,
With critters jiving, oh so grand.
Here in the light, let's all unwind,
Nature's joy, perfectly timed.

Shadows Whispering Untold Stories

In the shadows, whispers fly,
Secrets shared in a breezy sigh.
A raccoon's plot, a clever tease,
Nature's tales are meant to please.

A caterpillar dons a crown,
Pretending to be king of the town.
While loopy ants form a parade,
All joining in this grand charade.

Tall grasses bow, with a gentle roar,
Inviting all to the shadowed floor.
As twilight sneaks in with a wink,
The world giggles and begins to think.

What stories lie in every nook?
Plant your ears; come take a look.
For in the dim, laughter simmers,
In whispered shadows, joy just glimmers.

The Artistry of Nature's Hand

With brushes dipped in shades of green,
Nature paints scenes, so fresh and keen.
A masterpiece made without a plan,
Adding humor to every tree and span.

Clouds puff up like fluffy pies,
While flowers wink with playful sighs.
Breezes tickle, gently chime,
Nature's jests dance in perfect rhyme.

The sky is an artist, bold and bright,
Flinging colors from day to night.
Birds craft a symphony, wing to wing,
In this gallery, laughter is king.

So let's celebrate this joyful land,
Where every leaf is an artist's hand.
In Nature's joke, we play our part,
A fine display of the funny heart.

Echoes of the Silken Breeze

A squirrel danced in silly glee,
Chasing shadows, wild and free.
The leaves laughed in a playful breeze,
Tickling toes, with utmost tease.

A rabbit wore a tiny hat,
In search of snacks, he bumped a cat.
They shared a glance, a comic scene,
Both stunned by mischief, so routine.

Nearby a frog did croak and sing,
Reciting jokes, a gifted thing.
The owls rolled eyes, bemused all night,
As laughter echoed, pure delight.

So when you walk where antics play,
Expect the weird, come join the fray.
For in this realm of silly cheer,
Life's not too serious, let's be clear!

Sunbeams and Shadows Alike

A dappled sunbeam struck a tree,
Whispering secrets, oh so free.
The shadows laughed at silly pranks,
While leaves joined in with playful janks.

A butterfly lost in its dance,
Swirled past a bug, big chance romance.
They crashed, they tumbled, what a sight,
Fell into giggles, pure delight.

Under the branches, laughter spread,
As acorns dropped upon their head.
The sunbeams chuckled with a sway,
Inviting all to join the play.

So, dance with whimsy in your soul,
In nature's playground, feel the whole.
For here in shadows, bright and tame,
Life's a jest, and it's not the same.

Heartbeats Under the Canopy

A raccoon winks, a thief at heart,
Stealing snacks with crafty art.
The trees sway low, with knowing glance,
Join in the game, the food romance.

A parrot squawked a funny tune,
While nearby, frogs began to croon.
With silly hops and winged cheer,
They laughed so loud, we had to steer.

In this realm of silly strides,
Where laughter hops and humor glides,
Every heartbeat sings a rhyme,
Each joke timed, a big punchline.

So join the fun, and feel the beat,
In leafy realms, with joy, we greet.
For here beneath the leafy glow,
Life's a comedy, steal the show!

Serene Stand of Verdant Dreams

In the emerald depths where giggles bloom,
A hedgehog rolled to shake off gloom.
With tiny dance and prickle fight,
He twirled around, such pure delight.

Nearby a partridge pranced and strayed,
In search of crumbs her mate had laid.
She slipped and slid on leafy floor,
With flapping wings, she could not soar.

The trees erupted in gentle laughter,
As playful winds danced ever after.
Each rustling leaf shared a chuckle,
For nature's humor comes in muckle.

So wander here where jests are spun,
In greens and laughs, join in the fun.
For in this stand of dreams so bright,
Life's absurd, oh what a sight!

Dreams Cradled by Fronds

Beneath the leaves, a whispering sound,
A squirrel debates the best snack he's found.
The breeze carries giggles, oh what a tease,
As lizards dance jigs among swaying trees.

Crickets are drumming a late-night parade,
While fireflies wonder who stole their shade.
A raccoon, bemused, steals someone's drink,
With all of nature embracing a wink.

Dreams take flight on this leafy stage,
A deer prances by, all full of rage.
He thinks, 'These humans, they're quite absurd,
Believing my stealth can't be overheard.'

Coconuts drop like a clumsy old friend,
And the birds chime in with a laugh 'til the end.
Who knew here was such a carnival spree?
These fronds hold more joy than one might foresee!

Echoes of the Tropical Canopy

In the jungle where the sun likes to snooze,
Parrots gossip about their odd shoes.
A toucan tries to wear a hat so tall,
Yet ends up tangled, just a feathered squall.

The monkeys swing with all their bravado,
Planning a heist on the green avocado.
But slip and slide, and what a disgrace,
They tumble down, spread-eagled in space.

The sloth, with style, moves at a crawl,
Watches the chaos, not moved at all.
'Life moves fast,' he yawns, 'what a rush!'
As he sips on dew, all in no hurry but hush.

Echoes ring from this leafy delight,
Where laughter and goofiness take flight.
The canopy hums its hilarious tune,
Under the golden gaze of the cheeky moon.

Soulful Murmurs of the Jungle

In dappled light where shadows play games,
Frogs croak out ballads, calling out names.
The jaguar chuckles at a hasty hare,
'Why hurry, dear friend? It's not like I'm there!'

A parrot remarks with a sassy flair,
'You should've seen Fluffy, he grew quite the hair!'
As the slinky snakes laugh at this best,
Entangled in jokes, they are truly blessed.

The echoes of giggles embrace the green,
While turtles strut in a beauty routine.
Each leaf is a stage for the comic brigade,
Impressing the crowds with their own masquerade.

Under the quilt of the jade and the hue,
Life's playful antics dance like the dew.
Soulful mirth fills the jungle with cheer,
What a funny world, let's vivaciously steer!

The Breath of Lushness

In a jungle alive with whispers and glee,
A sloth on a vine has a view, oh so free.
He sings to the breeze with a lopsided smile,
While bees buzz around, thinking it's all worth the while.

A hippo floats by with a grin ear to ear,
Declaring the pond his own karaoke sphere.
'The lily pads rock and the water's just right,'
He croons to the cows as they chewed in delight.

Vines twist and curl like a wiggly worm,
As snakes play the game of who can squirm.
Pastel toucans flaunt their outrageous wear,
While laughing out loud at each other's despair.

The breath of lushness, a perfumed embrace,
Wraps all its critters in a whimsical chase.
In the vibrant green, everyone's a clown,
Under the sun, there's no frowny frown!

Serenity in the Hush of the Woods

A squirrel with a nut in tow,
Danced like no one else could know.
He tripped on roots and did a spin,
While birds all laughed, and passed him in.

A turtle judged from his slow lane,
Wondering why folks rushed through rain.
With every plod, he'd softly muse,
"Fast is fine, but slow's my muse!"

A raccoon in a picnic spree,
Wore crumbs as jewels, just like a spree.
He winked at me, a sly little prank,
In the woods, it's fun at every rank.

The whispers here are quite absurd,
As frogs croak out a funny word.
Nature's jokes, under trees they play,
Laughing leaves brighten up my day.

Lustrous Dreams in Nature's Snare.

A rabbit hops, quite out of luck,
His ears are stuck on a fishing truck.
"What's the catch?" he questions with zest,
"Just my carrot," the trucker confessed.

The fireflies start a tune so bright,
While ants march home in a funny sight.
They're all convinced they're in a parade,
Each step majestic, no need for trade.

A chipmunk juggles with seeds in tow,
His skills bring laughter, as jokes do flow.
"Who needs a circus? Just bring a tree!"
And in the woods, we giggle with glee.

On branches swaying like a dance,
Nature's humor, a leafy romance.
With whispers of joy in the night,
We dream of laughter, oh what a sight!

Whispers of Green Canopy

A woodpecker taps a silly tune,
"Hey, look at me!" he cries to the moon.
"Just don't blink or you might miss,"
His rhythm's a comedy, can't dismiss.

The branches sway with playful cheer,
While lizards sunbathe, muddled with beer.
They toast to bugs that run so fast,
In this sunny nook, oh what a blast!

A butterfly flutters with flair and style,
Dresses in colors that make us smile.
"Fashion week's here in the tree today!"
With every flap, it's nature's ballet.

As shadows play and laughter floats,
The whispers join like tiny boats.
In the green canopy's light embrace,
The world feels merry, a joyful space.

Secrets Beneath the Rustling Leaves

Beneath the leaves, a secret scout,
A snail says, "Life's a slow hangout!"
With a shell of colors, he rolls around,
Finding treasures on the ground.

A hedgehog wears a spiky cap,
Claiming it's best for a daytime nap.
With dreams of plump and juicy bugs,
He giggles softly, giving us shrugs.

In every rustle, a voice may sneak,
Lamenting ants that can't find a peak.
"Where are we off to?" they try to scheme,
In nature's game, there's always a dream!

So let us laugh as the wind does tease,
With nature's secrets whispered through trees.
Life is a joke, don't take it so deep,
Just share a smile, and tumble asleep.

Layers of Waiting Green

In shadows thick, the lizards play,
They dodge the drops of yesterday.
A caterpillar munches slow,
While ants debate on where to go.

The breeze whispers with silly sounds,
As if to tickle all the rounds.
Each leaf giggles in the light,
Celebrating their leafy plight.

The secret path of flowers bloom,
Where bees conspire to seal their doom.
They buzz and hiccup, what a sight,
Like tiny jesters taking flight.

Oh, waiting here is quite a jest,
With nature's humor as my guest.
Each moment stretched, a funny scene,
In layers soft, of waiting green.

An Invitation to Quietude

A gecko sings a tuneful rhyme,
While I sip tea and waste some time.
The trees nod off, so calm and still,
They dream of doing absolutely nil.

The breeze plays jokes on my wide hat,
It lifts it high, and then goes splat!
A squirrel laughs from yonder branch,
As I attempt my awkward dance.

The sun winks down with playful glee,
I wave it off, but it won't flee.
A gentle rustle, nature's cheer,
An invitation to stay right here.

So come and join this fun retreat,
Where laughter hops like tiny feet.
In quietude, we find the spark,
And giggle softly in the park.

The Song of Bark and Leaf

Bark whispers secrets to the leaves,
While ants throw parties, oh, how it weaves!
Each branch shakes hands with a passing breeze,
Inviting jokes, put minds at ease.

The sunbeams dance on leaves so bright,
Creating shadows that tease and bite.
A butterfly slips on the bark,
And giggles vanish into the dark.

The rhythm rolls like a gentle laugh,
While squirrels calculate their next path.
The song is strange, yet seems so good,
A melody played in the leafy wood.

From bark to leaf, the tales unfurl,
Laughter floats in this green world.
We join the chorus, merry and free,
In the joyful song of bark and leaf.

The Heart of a Tropical Dream

Beneath the sky, a tale unfolds,
With palm trees swaying, as it holds.
The sun is bright, a playful knave,
While shadows stretch, left in its wave.

A parrot laughs, with colors bold,
In feathers bright, a sight to behold.
It sings of mischief, of silly things,
Of floaty hats and unseen wings.

The breeze tickles as I sit and plot,
An ice cream cone, or maybe a lot!
The ants parade with snacks in tow,
While flowers bloom in a comic show.

In this tropical dream, we find delight,
Where laughter sparkles in daylight.
So join the fun, let the laughter beam,
In the heart of this tropical dream.

The Hush of Nature's Embrace

In a leafy castle, critters roam,
Chasing shadows, calling home.
A squirrel slips, and off he goes,
A comical tumble, villainous foes.

Whispering breezes share their jest,
As flowers giggle with nature's zest.
Each rustle's a punchline, a laugh in the air,
The trees join the chorus without a care.

Beneath the boughs, the world takes pause,
With acorns clattering, it gets applause.
Nature's stand-up, a show on repeat,
Life's little quirks can't be beat!

So let's raise a toast to the wild and free,
Where laughter and antics are the key.
In the hush of nature, hilarity flows,
In this leafy realm, anything goes!

Songs of the Wind-Kissed Foliage

Leaves sway gently, a mischievous crowd,
Dancing to secrets that make them loud.
A crow cracks jokes that soar through the air,
While worms in the soil are perfectly square.

Branches whisper tales of wise old trees,
Telling stories that flutter in the breeze.
A gust rolls through, hair in disarray,
Nature's confetti in a raucous display.

Bugs start a band, tuning up for a blast,
With a toad on the mic, singing songs from the past.
Each note a giggle, each chorus a cheer,
Nature's best comedy, perfectly clear.

So laugh with the rustles and sing with the thrum,
In this wild theater, there's never a glum.
Wind-kissed foliage, a stage for the brave,
Join in the laughter; it's true and it's grave!

Fragments of Calm in the Wilderness

Amidst wildflowers, mischief does bloom,
A rabbit sneezes, creating a boom.
Butterflies wink with a colorful flair,
While ants form a line for a picnic to share.

A frog cracks a joke, croaks it with glee,
His friends all just laugh; oh, what a spree!
The daisies droop, their heads in delight,
As the sun winks down, a comical sight.

Branches creak softly; they've heard it all,
The tales of the critters who've had a ball.
In quiet moments, there's laughter that swells,
Fragments of calm where humor excels.

So embrace the oddness, the whimsy, the fun,
In the wilderness, laughter's never done.
With a skip and a jump, join the wild spree,
In nature's sweet comedy, we all agree!

The Dance of Sun and Shade

Sunlight twirls, a playful sprite,
Casting shadows, oh what a sight!
The grass tickles toes, a soft embrace,
While the breeze throws leaves in a playful race.

In the dappled light, a funny old fox,
Struts like a model, flexing his socks.
Grasshoppers laugh, with a chirp and a leap,
In this sunlit studio, no one's asleep.

As rays weave stories, they twist and they sway,
Creating a stage for a madcap ballet.
Even the bunnies are hopping about,
Chasing their tails, giggles all throughout.

So come join the dance where the light is king,
With laughter and whimsy, let your heart sing.
In the dance of sun and shade, we're alive,
Finding joy in each moment, we thrive!

Enchanted Groves of Memory

In a forest full of pranks,
Trees wear hats made of twigs,
Squirrels play hide and seek,
Chasing their own silly jigs.

Noses twitch in the breeze,
Bees gossip in humming tunes,
While leaves play tricks on knees,
And mushrooms dance in the moons.

Laughter spills from the brook,
As frogs recite silly rhymes,
Each glance is a little look,
At playful moments in times.

Memory's laughter with bark,
Echoes in every light,
In groves with notes so stark,
Joy mingles with sheer delight.

Souls Entwined with Nature's Touch

The trees wink at the sun,
As petals wear their best smiles,
Birds in pajamas run,
On branches that sway in styles.

The wind throws a party,
With whispers and tickling air,
Carrying tales so hearty,
Of cows that dance without care.

Rabbits hop in fine coats,
While snails glide on their shells,
Underneath hats made of oats,
They share all their silly spells.

Nature's guffaws blend loud,
In a song only she knows,
All creatures join the crowd,
As laughter blooms and grows.

A Dance of Shadows and Light

Shadows waltz beneath beams,
A tango of mischief and cheer,
As sunlight plays tricksy dreams,
And giggles echo, oh so near.

Caterpillars in bow ties,
Owl in spectacles so grand,
They throw vibrant surprise,
In this wild and wacky land.

The sun plays peekaboo games,
Hiding behind clouds with a grin,
Nature's tapestry of flames,
Sparkling laughter from within.

A show of shadows in flight,
Twisting and turning with flair,
Each bounce a delightful sight,
Into the air, joy to share.

Nature's Secrets, Unveiled

In the woods where giggles bloom,
Fern fronds flutter to the beat,
Every corner hides a room,
With stories wrapped in sweet treat.

Turtles trade gossip with grace,
In slow-motion, they share their news,
And butterflies swirl in a race,
While bees do their dance with the blues.

Nature's stash of goofy charms,
Hides treasures with a touch of glee,
Every rustling whisper warms,
The hearts of those who dare to see.

So come, unveil this mirth,
Join the whimsy, feel alive,
In this secret laugh-filled earth,
Where the joys of nature thrive.

Murmurs of the Canopy's Heart

Underneath the leafy sky,
Squirrels plot their acorn heist.
Birds gossip with cheeky squawks,
While ants march with great advice.

The breeze whispers secrets low,
As shadows dance in playful jest.
A raccoon peeks with a sly grin,
Imagining all of us as guests.

Sunlight spills like golden tea,
Caught in laughter's sweet embrace.
Leaves wiggle, tickled by the wind,
Nature's joy, a cheeky grace.

Laughter echoes in the woods,
Where every branch has tales to share.
Delight skitters on tiny feet,
In this whimsical, leafy affair.

Flights of Fancy Amongst the Leaves

A feathered fellow takes to flight,
Spinning tales of daring deeds.
Leaves giggle in the afternoon,
As sunlight dances with their needs.

Bumblebees throw buzzing raves,
While ladybugs wink with delight.
Crickets compose symphonies,
In the glow of the dusk's soft light.

Oh, what jesters make their stage,
In the branches, high and free!
Unfurling all their leafy tricks,
Nature's comedy, wild and glee.

From misty dawn to twilight's glow,
The air is thick with jokes and cheers.
Each rustle entertains, it seems,
A giggling nature without fears.

Nature's Silent Conversations

Whispers float on invisible waves,
As beetles roll their tiny logs.
Caterpillars gossip on leaves,
Turning shy with passing fogs.

Moths with wings like painted dreams,
Debate the best spots to rest.
Branches sway like laughing friends,
While owls hoot their wise jest.

In the thicket, shadows play,
With secrets shared in the trees.
Laughter blooms in silent spaces,
Nature's humor dances with ease.

As moonlight bathes the land anew,
The forest chuckles, bold and bright.
Each rustle speaks of life's sweet quirks,
As stars twinkle with delight.

A Subtle Dance of Nature's Melody

In the twirl of rustling leaves,
Creatures prance with rhythm grand.
Chattering critters take a bow,
In this joyous, leafy band.

Dancing shadows, swift and spry,
Sway to whispers in the dark.
A parade of giggles fills the air,
As the dawn ignites a spark.

Grasshoppers leap with flair and style,
Sharing jokes in jumpy arcs.
The branches sway to nature's tune,
As the forest hums with larks.

A breeze joins the merry spree,
Encircling all in gentle jest.
In a world where laughter reigns,
Nature's melody is the best.

Chatters in the Canopy Above

A squirrel with acorns takes its aim,
Dodging the raindrops, oh what a game!
Chirpy bird gossip fills the air,
While monkeys swing, they've no time to care.

Lianas sway like a wobbly rope,
Clumsy sloths make viewers lose hope,
Laughing frogs leap with a splashy sound,
As nature's laughter echoes around.

A toucan's beak, so bright and bold,
Spills fruit juice like stories of old,
In this tall theatre of leaves and cheer,
Where every critter brings joy and beer!

Life's a fiesta, up in the trees,
Dancing with monkeys, if you please,
Under the canopy, so alive and free,
It's a party here, won't you join me?

Journey Through the Green Symphony

Beetles drum on a leaf with flair,
While high above, the parrots glare,
A symphony made of buzz and chirp,
A conductor's skill? Just a little blurb!

Frogs wearing tuxedos croak away,
Inviting ants to a fancy soiree,
Dancing in circles, tiny and round,
With dress shoes made of mud, they abound!

The trees sway gently with rhythm and rhyme,
Chasing the clocks, but never on time,
A jam session lost in leafy covers,
Where laughter's the tune underscoring lovers.

Lost in this melody, we'll sing and swing,
Join the parade, hear the laughter ring,
With every rustle, every fluttering leaf,
It's all just a jest, life's subtle relief!

A Tapestry Woven in Green

A tapestry hangs, made from laughter and twine,
Threads of bright antics, a true work divine.
Spotty leopards, they love to dance,
While the monkeys throw bananas for a chance.

With vines like ribbons, all tangled and tight,
A party unfolds under soft moonlight.
Breezy shenanigans float through the air,
Where every creature brings style and flair.

A weaving of stories, both silly and sweet,
Where even the tortoise can't help but beat,
The rhythm of life, so vibrant and free,
Come join this quilt, it's one big spree!

In this patchwork of joy, let's add some pizzazz,
From lizards to butterflies, it's all such a jazz!
Laughing together, we spin and we twine,
In this vivid jungle, we all intertwine.

Whirl of the Tropical Breeze

A whirlwind of giggles, a playful surprise,
As leaves swirl around, dancing improvise.
Chasing after butterflies, oh what a scene,
In this waltz with the wind, we're all so keen!

The breeze tells secrets to the cheeky chads,
As they whirl in circles, both happy and mad.
With every gust, a new game starts,
In this frolicsome land of wild little hearts.

The sun peeks in, tries to steal a glance,
But the shadows plot another chance,
Colorful mischief plays hide and seek,
In this frothy fun, we're all just unique!

A jolly parade in playful disguise,
Where every moment is filled with surprise,
So when the breeze whispers, take heed and please,
Join the laughter, in this tropical tease!

Secrets Held by Leafy Shadows

Whispers of secrets in the breeze,
Laughter is hidden among the trees.
A squirrel with secrets, oh what a tease,
In leafy shadows, time seems to freeze.

A ladybug giggles, feeling so sly,
Tickling the branches as they pass by.
The branches wave 'hello', oh my!
In the quiet, all creatures can't help but sigh.

Sunlight dances, a playful charade,
Chasing the giggles, never afraid.
In a world where fun is the only trade,
Let's join the game that nature has made.

So come, let's frolic, in this leafy dome,
With laughs and giggles, we feel at home.
Among the shadows where laughter can roam,
In leafy secrets, we'll forever comb.

Dreaming Under the Verdant Veil

Beneath the quilt of green so bright,
Dreamers gather, oh what a sight!
A raccoon with shades, a curious knight,
Plans out his dreams in the soft twilight.

Laughter erupts, soft as a sigh,
As chipmunks debate how high they can fly.
"Let's build a rocket!" they shout with a cry,
While a sleeping turtle winks with a sly eye.

The breeze brings jokes from blossoms so fair,
As dragonflies twirl in the fragrant air.
Each petal a giggle, whisking with flair,
In a realm of dreams, we're free of despair.

So let's dream on, in this leafy scene,
With whispers of joy, and visions serene.
In the shade of laughter, life's truly keen,
Under the veil of colors, we're never unseen.

Lulled by the Gentle Green

In a hammock of leaves, I sway and groove,
As the world spins round, I just want to move.
A sloth made me giggle, oh what a move,
Dreaming away in this leafy alcove.

The branches shimmy, an impromptu dance,
While fireflies twinkle, given the chance.
A butterfly whispers, "Join in the prance!"
As trees throw a party, we all take a glance.

The mushrooms chuckle, with hats oh so wide,
As fairies drop jokes, no reason to hide.
"Don't tell a rabbit, they jump while they glide,"
In the lull of the green, we've all got a ride.

So let's sway and giggle, in this gentle scene,
With laughter as bright as the freshest green.
In a world that's silly, where joy's evergreen,
The gentle green lulls, with smiles in between.

Dappled Sunlight's Serenade

Sunlight dapples with a wink and giggle,
As shadows play hopscotch, oh what a jiggle!
A frog serenades, with croaks that wiggle,
In a symphony of laughs, we all feel the wiggle.

The breeze joins in with its silly tune,
While spiders dance, waving glittery rune.
"Catch me if you can!" a butterfly croons,
In a game of chase, beneath the bright moon.

With laughter like petals, we scatter around,
In this sunlit joy, true magic is found.
A squirrel whispers jokes, profound yet quite sound,
In dappled sunlight, our hearts are unbound.

So come, let's gather, in this whimsical shade,
As giggles and beams in the sunlight parade.
With secrets of joy, in the dance we've made,
In this dappled serenade, we all won't trade.

Reflections Beneath the Gentle Boughs

Squirrels debate on the best nut,
While I sip tea and stifle a chuckle.
A bird in a tie, looking quite cut,
As he adjusts his wings, near some muck.

The sun laughs softly, casting its light,
On shadows that dance like they're in a show.
A butterfly twirls, what a curious sight,
While I wonder where all the silly bugs go.

Leaves whisper secrets to every breeze,
As a worm tries to wear a leaf as a hat.
I'm just here giggling, doing as I please,
Nature's antics are where the fun is at.

A raccoon steals berries, grinning so wide,
While I munch on snacks, a joy-filled feast.
Under leafy laughter, I blissfully bide,
In this green amusement, I've found my peace.

Nature's Palette in Shades of Green

A chameleon struts like it owns the scene,
Dressing in shades from chartreuse to jade.
I can't help but laugh, what an odd routine,
As it flashes its colors, unafraid.

In the tangle of vines, a lizard will slide,
Making faces that rival my own surprise.
While I chuckle, wide-eyed, and filled with pride,
At this wild performance, such sweet disguise.

The ferns wave hello, a synchronized dance,
With my toes tapping to the rhythm of fun.
I'd join them all there if given a chance,
And twirl around 'til the day is done.

Puddles can giggle when raindrops collide,
As frogs hop along, wearing coats of delight.
This nature's party, I'll abide by its guide,
Laughing and blending, all evening and night.

Choreography of the Wind's Caress

The branches sway like they're at a ball,
Inviting the clouds to join in the spree.
I watch in delight, laughing through it all,
As leaves do the limbo, wild and free.

With a twist and a turn, the breeze spins around,
As flowers waltz, peeking out to see.
A dancing delight in this nature-bound,
And I can't help grinning at this jubilee.

A dandelion spins with glee in the sun,
While bumblebees buzz like they've lost the plot.
Nature's own circus, a show full of fun,
And I'm just the audience, darling, who's not caught!

When the wind hits a high note, I join in the laugh,
Clapping for toads who leap with such grace.
In the theater of foliage, I take a paragraph,
Of humor and merriment, in this grand place.

Embracing Nature's Bounty

Apples hang high like they're on the edge,
A little squirrel scurries, eyes filled with cheer.
He leaps for a snack, then takes a pledge,
To avoid any humans, oh dear, oh dear.

The vines are a maze, a puzzle to crack,
While I lose the map, giggling through the fray.
Birds cheer me on as I take a step back,
And call out, 'Just wing it, it's the fun way!'

Under broad canopies, sunbeams play tricks,
As shadows do hopscotch with giggles and hops.
I can't help but snicker at nature's quick fix,
Mixing humor with bounty, my heart never stops.

A raccoon with flair shimmies for fun,
While I take a break with my jolly green drink.
Nature's own laugh track arrives with the sun,
Reminding me daily to smile, not to think.

www.ingramcontent.com/pod-product-compliance
Lightning Source LLC
Chambersburg PA
CBHW072130070526
44585CB00016B/1605